Symbolism and Discourses on the Entered Apprentice, Fellowcraft and Master Mason Blue Lodge Degrees

By H. L. Haywood, Asahel W. Gage, William Harvey, Albert G. Mackey and Arthur Edward Waite

Copyright © 2019 Lamp of Trismegistus. All rights reserved. No part of this publication may be reproduced or transmitted in any form or by any means, electronic or mechanical, including photocopying, recording, or by any information storage and retrieval system, without permission in writing from Hecate Arcanum. Reviewers may quote brief passages.

ISBN: 978-1-63118-413-0

Foundations of Freemasonry Series

Other Books in this Series and Related Titles

The Story and Legend of Hiram Abiff by William Harvey, Manly P. Hall and Albert G. Mackey (978-1-63118-411-6)

Symbolism of the Corner Stone, the North East Corner and the Religious & Masonic Symbolism of Stones by Albert G. Mackey, William Harvey and William Wynn Westcott (978-1-63118-412-3)

Ancient Mysteries and Secret Societies by Manly P. Hall (978-1-63118-410-9)

The Influence of Pythagoras on Freemasonry, the Golden Verses of Pythagoras and the Life and Philosophy of Pythagoras by Albert G. Mackey and Manly P. Hall (978-1-63118-320-1)

The Philosophy of Masonry in Five Parts by Roscoe Pound (978-1-63118-004-0)

Rosicrucian and Masonic Origins by Manly P. Hall (978-1-63118-000-2)

The Doorway of Freemasonry and the Mason's Apron by William Harvey (978-1-63118-001-9)

Four Lesser Known Masonic Essays by Frank C. Higgins (978-1-63118-003-3)

A Collection of Writings Related to Occult, Esoteric, Rosicrucian and Hermetic Literature, Including Freemasonry, the Kabbalah, the Tarot, Alchemy and Theosophy various authors *Volumes 1-4* (978-1-63118-713-1) (978-1-63118-714-8) (978-1-63118-715-5) (978-1-63118-716-2)

Audio Versions are also Available on Audible and iTunes

Table of Contents

Introduction...7

Studies in Blue Lodge Symbolism by H. L. Haywood...9

Symbolism of the First Degree by Asahel W. Gage...17

The Wages of an Entered Apprentice by William Harvey...25

Discourse on the Fellowcraft Degree by Arthur Edward Waite...35

The Legend of the Winding Stairs by Albert G. Mackey...43

The Third Degree: Its Ornaments and Emblems
by William Harvey ...57

Soliloquy For a Master Mason...73

Introduction

From the beginning of Modern Freemasonry's birthdate of 1717, the intelligentsia of humanity have found refuge for safe reflection within the walls of the fraternity. Masonic writers have produced a nearly incalculable amount of written musings on a multitude of esoteric and philosophical subjects, as they relate to the ancient mysteries that Freemasonry currently storehouses. Sadly, most of it appears to have sat largely unread, as American Freemasonry in particular, continues to transform itself into something that bears little resemblance to what it was originally designed to be. The true essence of Freemasonry is not that of blind patriotism or a single-minded national religion but one of Universal Brotherhood and altruism, designed for the betterment not just of its members but of society as a whole. In particular, for those who are not members of the fraternity, as Freemasonry has always acted as a beacon, to help guide humanity through darker times, with the hopes that one day we will collectively reach a truly enlightened age.

It's not uncommon for new members joining the fraternity to find little education within the walls of many modern lodges, in spite of so much written material available to the membership. Many older members are not simply uneducated with regards to real Masonic history and symbology, not to mention the vast arena of related subjects, but they are disinterested in all of it, as well.

Lamp of Trismegistus offers its readers highlights of Masonic study, culled from a variety of authors and viewpoints, with the hope bringing education back into the fraternity. So, be sure to check out other titles in our *Foundations of Freemasonry Series* as well as our *Esoteric Classics, Christian Apocrypha Series* and our *Theosophical Classics*, and don't be afraid to let a little altruism into your own heart or even into your Lodge.

Studies in Blue Lodge Symbolism

By H. L. Haywood

What are symbols? The simplest answer is to say that they are the storehouses in which wise men of the past have accumulated their wisdom. The assemblage of many symbols in our fraternity means that the fraternity is in itself a storehouse of the wisdom of many wise men. Wisdom can never be learned or taught by one man working alone; it is only when many men join their knowledge together that the truth is found. Many men in the past have wrought to discover truth; they have embodied their truths in symbols; in our Order these symbols are assembled together so that the wisdom of many wise men has been placed at our disposal; is not that a great privilege? Is it not a fine opportunity for those who desire to learn?

What do these symbols teach? It is not curious lore; it is not occultism; it is not information; it is the wisdom how to live; the purpose of Masonry as a whole is to teach men how to live and to help them to live and to learn how to live more and more. Each one of us needs to learn how to live; therefore Masonry has much to give to each one of us; we can help each other to learn how to live, therefore Masonry helps us to help each other. The symbols give us their wisdom, their light, their truth; we can receive this wisdom from them and we can then teach it to others. We can transform the dead symbol into life; that is the highest way to learn.

Why did the wise men of the past store their wisdom in symbols? Because, so we believe, symbols are forms of expression that never die. Language grows old and passes away; truth embodied in a language may become buried in the tomb in which the dead language lies. Books are not for the many; one cannot carry a book about with him in his mind. Institutions grow old and die; moreover, they cannot always be carried from country to country; truth embodied in institutions may become dead or lost to many. The teachers themselves have died and they could not themselves bring us their truth. There are many that cannot understand learned language; they need something very simple; they need to think in pictures; to think in pictures helps us all, because the mind seems to work that way. Symbols live on long after languages have died; symbols survive the wreck of institutions; they survive the teachers who have poured wisdom into them; they bring the truth to us in pictures so that all can conceive it; symbols are a deathless and universal language, the easiest to learn of all forms of language, the hardest to forget, the most packed with meaning. In teaching through symbols our Fraternity reveals itself as a very wise teacher. If the meaning of a symbol is often hidden from us that is to stimulate us to hunt for its meaning; hunting for its meaning develops our faculties; and the development of our faculties is one of the purposes and aims of wisdom.

To the man who has neither the eyes to see nor the will to work, Masonry seems to offer little; to him who will take the trouble to learn it has much to offer. Masonry holds rich gifts in its hands; are you willing to receive those gifts? You may if you are willing to study, to work, to develop. We have only that which we strive for; we possess only that which we earn; when truth is poured into a passive mind it is soon lost from that mind; when it is won by an active mind it becomes a part of that mind; when truth has become a part of the mind then is the mind truly cultured, for culture is that wisdom which has become a part of ourselves. Masonry helps to culture us by stimulating us to apply our mental powers to the study of those symbols in which many wise men have hidden truths so profound, so illuminating, so helpful, so packed with life. We ourselves, in this present hour, can best understand what symbols mean and how their meaning is to be discovered if we will turn to a few of them. Our selection may appear arbitrary, at first glance, but the meanings we shall win will fit themselves together into one lesson, into a truth that is one truth, the truth that wisdom is the learning how best to live, and that God helps each of us how best to live.

The beginning of wisdom is to develop ourselves; most of us have never discovered what are the possibilities of our own minds; we live poorly and meanly because we permit the highest powers to lie dormant; one is learning the wisdom of life when he strives to develop each power of himself to the uttermost. Of this the apron is the symbol. It means work; not manual work alone, but mental, and spiritual, and moral work also. The divinity of work; the divine necessity of work; the divine results of work; this is the truth taught us - through the apron. We are told that it is an older and nobler symbol than the Star, the Garter, the Roman Eagle. It is. God has been working from the beginning; to work is to do what God does; to do what God does is life. The apron teaches us one of the secrets of the divine life. It is not fame; it is not possessions; it is not pride, or lust for place or power; it is none of these things that deserve to stand as that which is the highest. The apron is higher than the symbols of these things because it is the symbol of the effort to develop ourselves; we can work on ourselves; we can work through ourselves; while we are working on and through ourselves we are then working to help others; to help others is God-like because God is always helping others. God Himself, in a certain deep sense, evermore wears the apron because He evermore works, works to help us, works to give us more and more life for evermore. What we make of ourselves is more important than what others make of us; how we use and develop ourselves is more important than what we possess or what reputation we may have. To work; to make the mind work, to make the body work, to make all things work together to give us life and to give others life, that is according to the will of God and the will of God is our life and our peace. He who wears the apron on his heart will become God-like because God's own heart is filled with labor on the behalf of all His worlds and all His children.

Many times our work asks of us that we sacrifice our ease, our pleasure, our place, or our money; he who is not willing to sacrifice the lesser for the sake of the greater has not yet learned wisdom; he does not yet know to live. Sacrifice is not to lessen our lives; it is to increase our lives; it surrenders the petty things in order that the greater things may more completely possess us; he who has become willing to give up the lower in order that the higher may be in him has learned wisdom, for wisdom is to learn how best to live.

The cross which appears so often through our ritual and in so many different forms has many different degrees of meaning but the one meaning running through all forms of the cross is that he who would learn to live must learn to surrender willingly the things that hinder life. Sacrifice, if we will but learn it, is our friend; it gives us more life and what gives us more life gives us more love and love is in itself friendship. The cross sometimes breaks the body in order that the soul may have its way; the cross sometimes bruises the mind in order that the spirit may more richly live; the cross helps while it seems to hinder; it heals when it seems to hurt. To learn to know when to sacrifice, how to sacrifice, what to sacrifice, and for what to sacrifice, that is wisdom, and wisdom is to know to live.

But life is not complete in any one of us; life lives in all men and each needs the life of all; when we share with others our life we are helping them to live; when we help others to live we become God-like because God continually gives life to all. Friendship is just the habit of giving our life to others; when we give our life away we possess more of it; the more we give the more we receive. This is the meaning of the clasped-hands, one of the most divine and beautiful of all our symbols. The life in me clasps hands with the life in you; my life joins its forces with your life; that makes more life. Brotherhood is the enrichment of life not for one's self alone but for all; brotherhood is God-like because God is the Great Brother of all men. His hands are clasped with ours and neither disaster nor death can break that clasp. When we clasp our brother's hand we clasp God's hand because God lives and works through our brother; when he clasps our hands he clasps God's hands because God lives and works through us. Brotherhood makes life rich, beautiful, and divine; brotherhood is the clearest revelation of God that we have. Brotherhood is love expressed toward our fellows; it is therefore divine because God is love.

Our system of symbols would be very incomplete if they did not give us this highest wisdom that God is love. The All-Seeing Eye reminds us that God sees far into the most secret depths of each of us; this means that God lives in us a part of our very selves else He could not know what is in us; God is love because He lives in each one of us. The altar reminds us that we can always and everywhere meet with God; He is never away from our hearts; He is never away from home; the human soul is His home. While we work, while we play, while we think, above all while we love, we are with Him; each moment can have its own altar; each place may have its shrine; the whole world is a meeting place between man and God; the whole earth may become an altar. The raising of the master in our third degree reminds us, depicts for us in an unforgettable symbol, that God is also eternal life; the master went into the grave but God went in after Him; we never die; there is no death; there is only change; we go on from life to life, ever and forever, and God ever helps us to go on from life to life. To know that God lives in us and that God is love helps us to lose all fears, the fear of disaster, of disgrace, of death; for where love is fear cannot be. The same eternal life which lived in the slain master lives also in us; God is continually willing to raise each of us from all our graves; from the grave of sloth, the grave of selfishness, the grave of hatred, of fear, of sorrow, of death. "Now have we eternal life"; always will we have eternal life. God is life and God is eternal. God is our life; therefore we are eternal.

Can there be, could there be, a teaching more wonderfully beautiful than this? Can you anywhere find a higher wisdom than this? This is the highest wisdom that we know how to live; God is our Life; to learn to live is to love God. Masonry teaches us that God is love; it teaches us how to love God. Masonry as a whole is one great symbol of men dwelling with God and God dwelling with men.

Symbolism of the First Degree

By Asahel W. Gage

In the beginning, the seeker for truth must be duly and truly prepared. In the usually accepted sense, this talk is unprepared. And yet, I spent five years in the "line" of the lodge observing, thinking about and studying Masonry. It is this study and my later contemplations that are my preparation to speak on the symbolism of the first degree.

It seems to me that the essence of every Masonic lesson is presented in the symbolism of the first degree. An entered apprentice is a Mason. The second, third, and so-called higher degrees are elaborations. All masonic business was formerly transacted in a lodge opened only on the first degree.

The Masonic lessons are practical lessons. They have a dollar and cents value. The Senior Warden tells us that he became a mason in order that he might receive master's, or larger, wages. That there may be no misunderstanding as to his meaning monetary wages, he further says, in order to "better support himself and family." If we will look honestly into our own hearts, we will see that we paid the price for the Masonic degrees because we hoped to receive the equivalent or a greater return. If we have not received a return equal to our original and annual investment, it is because we have not applied ourselves to the study of Masonry with freedom, fervency and zeal.

But let us understand each other. There is little chance of our making much headway unless we agree on a clear and definite meaning of the terms we use. It is not only good and pleasant, but it is necessary for us to dwell together in unity of thought, if we would arrive at a harmonious conclusion. We should therefore endeavor to clearly define our subject.

The word "symbol" is derived from the Greek, meaning "to compare." A symbol is the expression of an idea by comparison. Often, an abstract idea may be best conveyed by a comparison with a concrete object. A dictionary definition of a symbol would be, a sign or representation, which suggests something else.

Symbolism, therefore, is the science of symbols or signs, the philosophy or art of representing abstract truths and ideas by concrete things. Symbolism is suggestion; in sculpture and painting by form and color, in language by words, in music by sounds. What allegory and parable are in literature; what figurative speaking is in language; the same is symbolism.

The symbolism of the first degree is for the apprentice. An apprentice Mason is one who has begun the study of Masonry. Certain qualifications of a Masonic apprentice are a belief in a God, a desire for knowledge, and a sincere wish to be or service to his fellow creatures. Possessing these qualifications, the candidate follow a course of ancient hieroglyphic moral instruction, taught agreeably to ancient usages, by types, emblems and allegorical language. This is symbolism, and symbolism is universal language. It is the language in which God reveals himself to man. The manifestations of nature are only symbolic expressions of God.

Children learn best from symbols. Blocks and toys are crude symbolic representations of the more complicated things of life. Most of us learned our alphabet and almost everything else by the relationship or correspondence to things with which we were familiar. We are only children after all. Older children call themselves scientists and make their experiments in their laboratories. Each experiment is a symbol of what is taking place in the real world outside.

The apprentice in the moral science should give up the rags of his own righteousness and also all precious metals, symbolical of worldly wealth and distinction, and all baser metals, symbolical of offense and defense, in order that he may realize his dependence upon moral forces only. He should be clad in a garment signifying that he comes with pure intentions to learn the noble art and profit by its lessons, not to proselyte among others, but to develop and improve himself. He is carefully examined to ascertain whether he is worthy and well qualified to receive and use the rights and benefits of Masonry. Being satisfied that he is worthy and well qualified, he is admitted and is immediately impressed with the fact that he must undergo sacrifice and suffering if he would attain the end he seeks. Realizing that the good intentions of the candidate, his own righteousness or even the lodge organization, are not sufficient, we invoke the blessing and aid of God upon our search for knowledge and truth.

We follow the system of symbolism. When we would know the truth in regard to things too great for our minds to comprehend, we take as a symbol that which is within our mental grasp. We know that the truth about the things we cannot comprehend, is identical with the truth in relation to the symbol which we do comprehend.

The apprentice in his search for Light must start from the North with the Easter Sun in the East, and travel by way of the South to the West, and back into darkness. He again comes out of the North in the East and passes through the same course again and again in his development. Obstacles are met by the apprentice in his progress, so similar that they seem identical. The little occurrences of life may seem unimportant but they determine whether we will be permitted to advance. The apprentice must ever be worthy and well qualified.

The apprentice must advance on the square by regular upright steps. The symbolism is so common and universal that it is used in the slang of the street. Obligations are duties assumed. We must assume them if we would advance and having assumed them we are bound by them whether we will or not. Then the light breaks and we begin to see. We find that others, even the most learned, stand like the beginners. The Master is on a level with the apprentice, and extends a hand, which is grasped fraternally, and the candidate is raised. There is the key to the Masters Word -- an open book, but he may never find the word itself.

Then, as before, the apprentice must follow the course of the Sun. As is the greatest, so is the smallest. In the drop of water are all the laws of the universe. If we study carefully, we will find in the dew drop the particles revolving and whirling in their little circles the same as we find the heavenly bodies revolving and turning in their great orbits, circle within circle and circle upon circle. The seeker after Light always emerges from the North in the East and passes by way of the South to the West and again into darkness, with full faith and perfect confidence that day will follow night. He is continually subjected to tests and trials and always held responsible for what he has learned and for that which has gone before.

God's Holy Book, His revelation to us, is the guide in our search for light. To the Jew this Holy Book is the history of Israel, substantially the Old Testament. To the Christian, it is the Old and New Testament. To the Muslim, it is the Koran; to the Hindu, the Veda. But whatever book it is, it is the Holy Book of the seeker for Light and that which he believes to be the word of God. The Holy Book together with the square and the compasses are the great lights of Masonry.

The lesser lights are the Sun, Moon and Master of the Lodge. The Sun symbolizes the great active principle, the Moon the great passive principle. This symbolism is so commonly accepted that even the uninitiated refer to the Sun as masculine and the Moon as feminine. The Master is symbolical of the offspring of the great Active and Passive Principles. He is the mediator, the child of the two great forces. He sets the craft to work upon their symbolic studies, which is no light responsibility to be assumed by the uninformed. Only chaos and disaster can overtake him who attempts the work he is not qualified to perform. When the apprentice has received his degree he is given his working tools and primary or elementary instructions as to how to go to work.

The working tools of an apprentice are the 24-inch gauge and the common gavel. The gavel symbolizes strength or force. Force undirected is the flood devastating all in its path or the idle puff of the unconfined powder, which accomplishes nothing. Undirected force is the gavel without the rule. But intelligently controlled, and directed along a proper line by the rule of intellect, the force of the torrent grinds the grain and does the work of many men. The force of the exploding powder pries the rock loose so that the work of months is accomplished in a moment.

The operation of universal laws in the moral world is just as ascertainable and understandable as in the physical world. Morals are as susceptible of scientific study as physics.

The lambskin apron, a most ancient symbol, signifies that it is only by honest conscientious toil that the moral laws can be learned and applied, and that this toil must be done in purity and innocence.

In the lectures, which follow the ceremony of the first degree, the apprentice is given preliminary information. It would be too tedious to analyze these lectures at this time. Suffice it to say they are very superficial and of little worth in themselves. They must be understood and felt, if they are to be of any value. Briefly we may describe a Lodge as a place to work, a place to study, analyze, and master the moral science so that we may make use of the moral laws and principles in our everyday life. Symbolically, it is representative of the world, our daily working place.

The foundation of the Lodge and its teaching is squareness. It is, however, supported by three pillars; Wisdom, Strength and Beauty. From which we may learn that in every undertaking, when intelligence or wisdom directs, and strength or power works, then beauty and harmony result.

The Lodge is covered with the blue vault of Heaven. Blue is the symbol of equality, it is a proper mingling of all colors, and it is in perfect concord. It is also symbolical of the universality of that charity, which should be as expansive as the blue vault of Heaven itself. Charity is not the giving of money alone; it is also necessary to have charity toward the weaknesses and mistakes of others.

This life is a checkered pavement of good and evil, but in the center is the blazing star, which is the seed and the source of all life and eternal life.

The parallel lines have a symbolism analogous to that of the two pillars, Jachin and Boaz, which is more fully developed in other degrees. The point in the center of the circle between the parallels is sometimes compared to the individual member and sometimes to God who is the center of all things. The circumference may suggest the boundary of man's conduct, or God's creatures, all equally distant and all equally near to Him. Sometimes the circumference is used to depict the endless course of god's power, and His existence without end. This is all speculation, it is symbolism, the contemplation of which will develop the individual.

If the apprentice pursues his studies in the moral art with freedom, fervency and zeal, he will receive Master's, or large wages, and be thereby the better enabled to support himself and family and to contribute to the relief of the distressed.

The Wages of an Entered Apprentice

By William Harvey

The Catechisms of the Craft and the conventional Lecture on the Tracing Board of the Second Degree, all of which speak with that authority which belongs to age, tell us that the Wages of an Entered Apprentice are Corn, Wine, and Oil. Sometimes it is added that he received Corn for food, Wine for nourishment, and Oil for comfort. The broad difference that was sought to be set up between the Apprentice and the Fellowcraft apparently was that the Fellowcraft was paid in coin while the Apprentice was paid in kind. I fear it would be very difficult to produce any authority for this, and probably the distinction between the Masons of the two degrees is the invention of some imaginative brother who ma have got the hint from a practice that was not uncommon among early operatives. Two or three centuries ago the conditions of labor were laid down as firmly as they are today by our powerful Trades Unions. A master could not employ more than a certain very limited number of apprentices-often the number was restricted to one-and these apprentices were taken bound to serve their masters for a period of seven years. Not infrequently, alike in mason and other trades, the apprentice went into residence with his master, and during the early years of his apprenticeship received no remuneration except board and lodging. Only when he became a journeyman, or Fellowcraft, and was free from the master who had taught him his business, was he entitled to wages in the form of cash. If, as is possible, some elaborator of Freemasonry, got the hint here as to the remuneration of an apprentice, one can easily understand that commonplace language such as "board and lodging" would not appeal to him and that he would seek to ornament the matter with just such a combination of words as "Corn, Wine, and Oil."

One of the traditions of the Craft, dearly beloved by uncritical Freemasons, says that the whole number of workmen engaged on the Temple at Jerusalem amounted to 217,281 persons, and that of these, 80,000 were Fellowcrafts, and 30,000 were Entered Apprentices-the latter of whom were arranged into one hundred lodges with three hundred members in each. This immense multitude was paid weekly on the sixth day of the week; and one tradition solemnly asserts that the 80,000 Fellowcrafts toiled up the Winding Stair to the Inner Chamber to receive their wages. Mackey tells us in his "Lexicon" that the Fellowcrafts "were paid in corn, wine, and oil," and the authors of "The Reflected Rays of Light upon Freemasonry," adopting the same view say, "What could be more absurd than to believe that eighty thousand craftsmen had to ascend such a stair, to the narrow precincts of the Middle Chamber to receive their wages in corn, wine and oil?" It is very evident that Mackey and the authors of "Reflected Rays" have misread the Lecture on the Second Tracing Board. It was the Entered Apprentice who received the corn, wine, and oil, and wherever he got it, he did not receive it in the Inner Chamber. To gain access to that apartment a workman required the pass-grip and password of a Fellowcraft, and it is obvious that no Entered Apprentice could have possessed these.

One may pause here for a moment to remark that, according to another tradition all the workers of every degree were paid in current coin. The total wages bill is alleged to have amounted to about 140,000,000 Pounds Sterling, and it was distributed among the craftsmen on a progressive scale which was quite obviously adjusted on the principle of the more honor the more pay. At the one end of the industrial line stood the humble Entered Apprentice who received one shekel, or about 2s 3d of English money per day, while, at the other end, was the Super-Excellent Mason who received 81 shekels per day, equal to about 9- 2s 3d sterling. One Masonic author very generously describes this as "only a fanciful speculation of some of our ancient brethren," and we may return, therefore, to our Corn, Wine, and Oil.

If I am right in my theory that the Wages of an Entered Apprentice in Speculative Freemasonry were suggested by the board and lodging which were the reward of the Operative youth while learning his trade, I think it is clear that the person who fixed the Wages of the Speculative Apprentice found his material in the Volume of the Sacred Law. We read in the Second Chapter of the Second Book of the Chronicles that, when Solomon appealed to the King of Tyre for assistance in building the Temple, he said, "Behold, I will give to thy servants, the hewers that cut timber, twenty thousand measures of beaten wheat, and twenty thousand measures of barley, and twenty thousand baths of wine, and twenty thousand baths of oil." The offer of Solomon was accepted by the King of Tyre, who replied, "Now, therefore, the wheat, and the barley, the oil, and the wine, which my lord hath spoken of, let him send unto his servants: and we will cut wood out of Lebanon, as much as thou shalt need." The account preserved in the fifth chapter of the First Book of the Kings, indicates that the gifts were made annually to Hiram's work people, but there is a discrepancy as to the amount. In 1st Kings the Wine is omitted, and the Oil is set down at "twenty measures" equal to about 1640 gallons, whereas the 20,000 baths of 2nd Chronicles were more than ten times as much, being the equivalent of about 165,000 gallons.

It is clear that these gifts of Corn Wine, and Oil were made to the hewers of wood in the forests of Lebanon, none of whom were Entered Apprentice Masons, but it would be unprofitable and useless to linger upon a discussion of the matter, as the Wages of the First, Degree in Speculative Freemasonry are merely symbols upon which to meditate, and from which to draw inspiration for everyday duties.

Corn, Wine, and Oil were the three staple crops of the Holy Land, and each of them entered into the fiber of the national life, furnishing figures of speech for the Hebrew poets, and points for the proverbs of the people.

Corn was always regarded as an element of national wealth. It formed part of the tribute brought to Hezekiah on the restoration of the priesthood. Bread was one of the signs of welcome and goodwill to Abraham.

Wine, in a metaphorical sense, represents the essence of goodness. Jerusalem, Israel, the Messiah, the righteous - all are compared to wine. The wicked are likened unto vinegar, and the good man who turns to wickedness is compared to sour wine. An abundance of wine was regarded as an indication of prosperity. Jacob blessed Judah that "he washed his garments in wine, and his clothes in the blood of grapes." We read in the ninth chapter of Judges that, when the trees went forth to anoint a King, they said unto the vine, "Come thou, and reign over us;" whereupon "the vine said unto them, Should I leave my wine, which cheereth God and man, and go to be promoted over the trees?" A writer in the "Jewish Encyclopedia" says that as wine "cheereth God" no religious ceremony should be performed with other beverages.

Oil was one of the most important and perhaps the most characteristic of the products of Palestine. It is mentioned no fewer than two hundred times in the Bible and, with one exception, the references are to "olive oil," as it is expressly termed in Exodus and Leviticus, according to the more correct rendering of the Revised Version of the Scriptures. Oil was largely used in the preparation of different kinds of food, and it was spread upon bread very much in the same way as we use butter; it was employed in the lighting of houses and places of worship-that used in the Temple being no doubt of the finest quality like the "beaten oil" for the Tabernacle - and it occupied a very prominent place in the ceremonial of anointing kings and priests- The metaphorical uses of the word "oil" are many. Part of the blessing of Asher was that he should "dip his foot in oil," that is, that he should have a large measure of worldly prosperity by finding abundance of oil within his territory. In the book of the Proverbs we find the foolish use of oil quoted as a token of extravagance and a source of poverty, while the husbanding of it is a certain proof of wisdom. Words of deceit are said to be smoother and softer than oil; and cursing is said to permeate the life of the wicked even as oil soaks into bone. The power and use of oil are illustrated in many ways in sacred writings. The scholars of Palestine were often referred to as "sons of oil." One injunction has a singularly poetic fancy about it: "Ye shall take olive oil to light the Temple as an atonement for your souls which are like to lamps" The yoke of Sennacherib was said to have broken "because of the oil which Hezekiah lighted in the schools;" and we have a singular parallel to this in the saying of one of the early English reformers who, when Ridley was burned at the stake, exclaimed: "Thou hast lighted such a fire in England to-day, Master Ridley, as shall not be put out." One common and significant use of Oil in Palestine was that of anointing the heads of guests entertained at a festive meal, and from this daily custom oil came to be regarded as a symbol of joy and gladness.

The Wages of an Entered Apprentice constitute the Masonic elements of consecration. Corn, Wine, and Oil figure very prominently in the elaborate ceremonial by which buildings are solemnly set apart and dedicated to the purpose of Freemasonry. After appropriate exercises of prayer and praise, the junior Warden, handing the Cornucopia to the consecrating Master, says: "In the dedication of Masonic Halls, it has been of immemorial custom to pour corn upon the Lodge in token of the divine goodness exhibited in the liberal provision made for all our wants, spiritual and temporal. I, therefore. Present to you this vessel of corn, to be employed by you according to use and wont." The Master thereupon accepts the vase and, sprinkling some corn upon the floor,- says: "In the name of the great Jehovah, to Whom be all glory, I do solemnly dedicate this Hall to Freemasonry."

Thereafter the Senior Warden presents the Vase with Wine, saying: "Right Worshipful Master, Wine, the symbol of strength and gladness, having according to ancient custom been used by our brethren in the dedication and consecration of their Lodges, I present to you this vessel of Wine, to be used on the present occasion according to established Masonic form." And the Master, sprinkling some of the wine upon the floor, says: "In the name of the Holy Saint John, I do solemnly dedicate this Lodge to Virtue."

Finally, the Substitute Master approaches with the vase containing Oil and says: "Right Worshipful Master, I present to you, to be used according to ancient custom, this vessel of oil, an emblem of that joy and peace which should animate every bosom on the completion of every important undertaking." And the master, sprinkling some oil upon the floor, says: "In the name of the whole Fraternity, I do solemnly dedicate this Lodge to Universal Benevolence."

In ancient days Corn, Wine, and Oil constituted the wealth of the people, and were esteemed as the main supports of life. The Psalmist counts them among the greatest blessings mankind enjoys, and you may recall that he brings them together in the 104th Psalm where he speaks of them as "Wine that maketh glad the heart of man, and oil to make his face to shine, and bread which strengtheneth man's heart." It is sometimes said that modern Freemasonry is but ancient sun-worship disguised. We believe in a beneficent Creator; the sun worshipper paid his adorations to the glorious luminary of the day to whose genial agency the fruits of the earth -corn, wine, and oil -were due. To that extent we have a community of thought, and Freemason and sun-worshipper alike look from Nature up to Nature's God.

Moralizing upon the Wages of the Entered Apprentice as symbols instinct with meaning to the Mason who would be true to the altruistic spirit of the Craft, the Rev. Thaddeus Harris says: "Wherefore my brethren do you carry Corn Wine, and Oil, in your processions, but to remind you, that in the pilgrimage of human life you are to impart a portion of your bread to feed the hungry, to send a cup of your wine to cheer the sorrowful, and to pour the healing oil of your consolation into the wounds which sickness hath made in the bodies, or affliction rent in the hearts of your fellow-travellers."

And surely brethren, that is the sum and substance of the matter. As Entered Apprentices we receive these Wages in spirit, not to expend upon ourselves but as a constant source of aid to our less fortunate Craftsmen. As Corn is an emblem of Plenty, let us be abundant in the measure of our brotherly love, ever ready to use what means God hath given us to assist a brother who may claim our help. As Wine is an emblem of Cheerfulness, let us foster the spirit of joy and gladness so that, when sorrows throw their shadows upon life, we may be enabled to look forward to the brighter day when the trials of our earthly pilgrimage shall be forgotten, and sadness shall be unknown. And as Oil is an emblem of Peace may it be ours to extend the boundaries of her Empire, so that strife and discord may be banished forever from the mind of man. "Nothing," says Emerson in one of his Essays, "nothing can bring you peace but yourself. Nothing can bring you peace but the triumph of principles." And this personal note is emphasized in a striking passage in one of Ruskin's "Lectures." "People," he says, "are always expecting to get peace in heaven, but you know whatever peace they get there will be ready made. Whatever making of peace they can be blest for, must be on the earth here." The whole teaching of the Craft is the promotion of peace on earth, goodwill to men, and it is the personal duty of every one of us to advance the cause of the universal brotherhood of man.

Brethren, I do not know that any one could leave a sweeter memory behind him than just this that he had faithfully used the Wages of an Entered Apprentice. The day will come when the walls of our Lodge shall know us no more, and we shall live in the recollection of our fellows for but a little while - a month, a year, at the most a generation. But that recollection will be a sacred one if those with whom we have labored recall our names from time to time, and tell those who did not know us that, faithful to our trust, we were ever ready to relieve distress, aid the weak, and comfort the mourner. Thus shall we have proved our right to the Wages of an Entered Apprentice, and thus may we hope for the recognition that awaits all faithful Craftsmen at the hands of the Great Architect of the Universe.

Discourse on the Fellowcraft Degree

By Arthur Edward Waite

Brethren of the Order, and those among you in particular who have been received recently among us, there is no period too early to conceive a just and commensurate notion of the great institution to which we belong, and in which we have been incorporated as a part of its living body. It is desirable, in the first place, that we should understand certain intimations which occur in the Grade of Neophyte and in that of Fellow Craft. They are open on their surface to misconstruction, and did we afterwards pursue our researches into the history of Emblematic Freemasonry, it might even be thought that they were untrue unless we carried them further than is done commonly. Moreover, in the absence of such researches, they might come to be regarded as so many figures of speech.

The Entered Apprentice is told at an early stage of his experience that the Order possesses great and inestimable privileges as well as those secrets and mysteries concerning which he is sworn to inviolable secrecy. You will observe that the privileges are enumerated separately from the secrets, though the latter stand also for privileges. Among these I will particularize the Signs and Words of the successive Degrees. The privileges imparted by these include the right of entrance to a Lodge, as a guest or subscribing member. They are the titles of our initiation and assuredly they are more than valuable after their own kind, but they do not respond in themselves to the very wide claim which I have mentioned. I conceive therefore that there are other privileges. These are not, however, to be identified with the things implied by the great principles of the Order, precious as are the latter to our hearts, and advantageous as it must ever be to dwell within a circle of fellowship which recognizes the principles of solidarity and will at need extend them in good will to us. They are not in the category of those things which we seek to reserve to worthy men alone. They are rather the marks, seals and characters which it is our sacred duty to display and by which Masonry is known all over the world in its practice of beneficence, benevolence and fraternity, by the love of moral truth and by the truth which abides in honor. I conclude, therefore, that the reference to inestimable privileges is itself in the nature of a mystery and covers things, which do not exactly appear on the literal side of our rituals. This is the first point which I am now seeking to commemorate.

The second is concerned more especially with the obligation of the Neophyte Grade in which the Candidate is pledged to hele, conceal and never reveal the secret art and hidden mysteries of Masonry. I believe that after a little reflection I shall carry with me the concurring voice of every Brother amongst us, if I say that this pledge, with the penalties attached thereto, must cover more than the simple signs, tokens, words and procedure which takes place in our Lodges, or too elaborate machinery may be thought to be put in motion than the-end appears to require. Hence again it seems certain that the reference to secret arts and hidden mysteries is itself in the nature of a mystery and covers things which do not precisely appear on the literal surface of our Rituals. This is the next point, which I am seeking to commemorate here.

For the third, we must pass from the Grade of Initiate or Neophyte to that of Fellow Craft, in which there is a brief but singularly pregnant account (1) of that which was attained by the Candidate when he was made an Entered Apprentice; and (2) of that which he is expected to perform in his new capacity as a Craftsman. In the one it is pointed out that he has made himself acquainted with the principles of moral truth and virtue. Now, this is literally true, subject to a single reserve: as one newly admitted, he was not intended to be tried beyond his strength: the principles which he is said to have acquired were in reality communicated to him without action on his own part, but he was left in the First Degree to reflect upon them. They are actually the root matter and sum total of moral truth and all natural virtue. It is otherwise in the Degree of Fellow Craft. There it is assumed that the Masonic horizon has opened before and about him, and that he is prepared to enter an almost immeasurable region. He is accordingly advised (1) that he is expected to make the liberal arts and sciences his future study, and (2) that he is permitted to extend his researches into the hidden mysteries of nature and science. Once again, this is an intimation which covers much more than appears on the literal surface and is a mystery which is expressed shortly but not explained in our Rituals. Here is the third point which I am now seeking to commemorate.

Let us see if there is any direction in which we can turn for a little light on these problems, and as it so happens we shall not have to go outside the Lodge itself.

On his first entrance into Freemasonry the newly received Brother will perceive that he has come into a world of emblems or symbolism, and that whatsoever takes place therein has a meaning behind it which is by no means indicated invariably on the surface. Sometimes, and indeed frequently, there is more than one inward meaning, depending on the point of view from which it is approached. The Lodge is an eloquent example of this truth. When its door opens for the Candidate he enters into an institution, which has its branches spread over the four quarters of the globe. It may be a very small Lodge: it may be a Lodge of poor Brothers only: but whosoever is received therein is recognized through the Masonic world, in all countries and among all peoples. But there is more even than this: however humble in its appointments and proportions, that Lodge is a Microcosm, a symbol, a speaking likeness of universal Freemasonry. It represents also and contains the life of Masonry, and the Ceremony of his initiation integrates the newly-made Brother in that peculiar quality of life which is the principle and essence of the Order. He becomes part of an organic whole. In the third place, the Lodge is held to represent the three dimensions of space--that is to say, the universe itself as a cosmos: in length from East to West, in breadth between North and South, in depth from the surface to the center, and even as high as the heavens.

It is therefore as if the Candidate on his initiation had been born anew into the universe, or that a door had opened to admit him into another cosmos. He comes with his eyes dim and with a restraint about him; he is kept for a considerable period in a state of darkness and bondage: ultimately he is instructed, and that which he finds about him is truly the symbolic representation of a new world. For him at that moment all things seem to be renewed, and it is very soon after this strange and wonderful experience that he is given a key to the meaning. He is told that he is the corner stone of a new foundation, from which he has to build up himself after another and higher manner. In other words, he has to remake his inward nature according to the perfection of the standard which is prescribed by Masonry. It is a moral standard in respect of his dealings with his Brethren and with mankind at large. It is a spiritual standard in respect of his duty towards God, and through obedience thereto it is hoped, held and known that he will ascend to the home of the spirit in the heavenly kingdom, by means of the ladder of Jacob, the successive rounds of which are called by many names, but chief among these are faith, hope and charity. It follows that he has a two-fold work to perform, but it is all in the training of himself. If he be successful, the result will be perfect in its parts and honorable to the builder. From this point of view, the just, perfect and regular Lodge is also a symbol of the man in that state which he is called to attain.

Now, the word initiate, with which we are so familiar in Masonry, signifies a person who has made a new beginning, who has entered a path of experience heretofore untraveled. Its equivalent in other orders and fraternities is the word Neophyte. The Neophyte is also one who has made a new beginning and the term, which is Greek in its origin, signifies him who is reborn, a new plant, one who is remade. In the old instituted mysteries, like those of Samothrace, of Egypt and of Eleusis, the Candidate was regenerated or reborn-- he was otherwise transferred or grafted--at the beginning of his experience, and afterwards he passed through successive stages of a new life till he attained the culminating Grade. It was the same experiment as that of Craft Masonry, in which the Candidate-- as an Entered Apprentice--lays the foundation stone of that new building which is himself, raises a super structure according to the law and order that Masonry has imposed upon him, continues the erection as a Craftsman, in which Degree the mysteries of Nature and science, recommended to his study, are mysteries of God and the estimation of His wonderful works till at last he puts on the capstone when the Lodge is open in the Sublime Grade of Master.

Our secret art is therefore an art of life, an art of perfection, an art of creation according to a prescribed standard recognized in Masonry: our hidden mysteries are those of our own relations to God, man and the universe, that we may be enabled to fulfill by Masonry the higher law of our being. The inestimable privileges of Masonry include those of its symbolism, the study of which is for our instruction in this high mode of self-building. The arts and mysteries which we are pledged to conceal from the profane are also those of the peculiar law of life in Masonry by which these ends can be reached. Those who are outside the Lodge must come within it, if they desire to share in that life. It is really incommunicable beyond the mystic circle, for the simple reason that it is life itself and not one of its substitutes. While therefore we are properly pledged concerning it, there is something which we could not impart even if we tried. In some of the old mysteries, from which we are indirectly descended, initiation and its sequels meant real instruction in this subject, and several of our most suggestive intimations are reflections from that remote source.

And seeing that the Grade of Master Mason is not so much a reflection as the very root, essence and quintessence, of those mysteries, and may be shortly described as an experiment in the deep mystery by which the soul passes through mortal life towards that life in God which is the end of all the mysteries, it comes about in this manner, my Brethren, that we are incorporated with all the great orders and sodalities of the far past and are therefore justified when we say that the meaning of our Masonic Badge is more ancient than the Golden Fleece and that our honorable institution--though under many transformations--has subsisted from time immemorial.

The Legend of the Winding Stairs

By Albert G. Mackey

Although the legend of the Winding Stairs forms an important tradition of Ancient Craft Masonry, the only allusion to it in Scripture is to be found in a single verse in the sixth chapter of the First Book of Kings, and is in these words: "The door for the middle chamber was in the right side of the house; and they went up with winding stairs into the middle chamber, and out of the middle into the third." Out of this slender material has been constructed an allegory, which, if properly considered in its symbolical relations, will be found to be of surpassing beauty. But it is only as a symbol that we can regard this whole tradition; for the historical facts and the architectural details alike forbid us for a moment to suppose that the legend, as it is rehearsed in the second degree of Masonry, is anything more than a magnificent philosophical myth.

Let us inquire into the true design of this legend, and learn the lesson of symbolism which it is intended to teach.

In the investigation of the true meaning of every masonic symbol and allegory, we must be governed by the single principle that the whole design of Freemasonry as a speculative science is the investigation of divine truth. To this great object everything is subsidiary. The Mason is, from the moment of his initiation as an Entered Apprentice, to the time at which he receives the full fruition of masonic light, an investigator—a laborer in the quarry and the temple—whose reward is to be Truth. All the ceremonies and traditions of the order tend to this ultimate design. Is there light to be asked for? It is the intellectual light of wisdom and truth. Is there a word to be sought? That word is the symbol of truth. Is there a loss of something that had been promised? That loss is typical of the failure of man, in the infirmity of his nature, to discover divine truth. Is there a substitute to be appointed for that loss? It is an allegory which teaches us that in this world man can only approximate to the full conception of truth.

Hence there is in Speculative Masonry always a progress, symbolized by its peculiar ceremonies of initiation. There is an advancement from a lower to a higher state—from darkness to light—from death to life—from error to truth. The candidate is always ascending; he is never stationary; he never goes back, but each step he takes brings him to some new mental illumination—to the knowledge of some more elevated doctrine. The teaching of the Divine Master is, in respect to this continual progress, the teaching of Masonry—"No man having put his hand to the plough, and looking back, is fit for the kingdom of heaven." And similar to this is the precept of Pythagoras: "When travelling, turn not back, for if you do the Furies will accompany you."

Now, this principle of masonic symbolism is apparent in many places in each of the degrees. In that of the Entered Apprentice we find it developed in the theological ladder, which, resting on earth, leans its top upon heaven, thus inculcating the idea of an ascent from a lower to a higher sphere, as the object of masonic labor. In the Master's degree we find it exhibited in its most religious form, in the restoration from death to life—in the change from the obscurity of the grave to the holy of holies of the Divine Presence. In all the degrees we find it presented in the ceremony of circumambulation, in which there is a gradual inquisition, and a passage from an inferior to a superior officer. And lastly, the same symbolic idea is conveyed in the Fellow Craft's degree in the legend of the Winding Stairs.

In an investigation of the symbolism of the Winding Stairs we shall be directed to the true explanation by a reference to their origin, their number, the objects which they recall, and their termination, but above all by a consideration of the great design which an ascent upon them was intended to accomplish.

The steps of this Winding Staircase commenced, we are informed, at the porch of the temple; that is to say, at its very entrance. But nothing is more undoubted in the science of masonic symbolism than that the temple was the representative of the world purified by the Shekinah, or the Divine Presence. The world of the profane is without the temple; the world of the initiated is within its sacred walls. Hence to enter the temple, to pass within the porch, to be made a Mason, and to be born into the world of masonic light, are all synonymous and convertible terms. Here, then, the symbolism of the Winding Stairs begins.

The Apprentice, having entered within the porch of the temple, has begun his masonic life. But the first degree in

Masonry, like the lesser Mysteries of the ancient systems of initiation, is only a preparation and purification for something higher. The Entered Apprentice is the child in Masonry. The lessons which he receives are simply intended to cleanse the heart and prepare the recipient for that mental illumination which is to be given in the succeeding degrees.

As a Fellow Craft, he has advanced another step, and as the degree is emblematic of youth, so it is here that the intellectual education of the candidate begins. And therefore, here, at the very spot which separates the Porch from the Sanctuary, where childhood ends and manhood begins, he finds stretching out before him a winding stair which invites him, as it were, to ascend, and which, as the symbol of discipline and instruction, teaches him that here must commence his masonic labor—here he must enter upon those glorious though difficult researches, the end of which is to be the possession of divine truth. The Winding Stairs begin after the candidate has passed within the Porch and between the pillars of Strength and Establishment, as a significant symbol to teach him that as soon as he has passed beyond the years of irrational childhood, and commenced his entrance upon manly life, the laborious task of self-improvement is the first duty that is placed before him. He cannot stand still, if he would be worthy of his vocation; his destiny as an immortal being requires him to ascend, step by step, until he has reached the summit, where the treasures of knowledge await him.

The number of these steps in all the systems has been odd. Vitruvius remarks—and the coincidence is at least curious—that the ancient temples were always ascended by an odd number of steps; and he assigns as the reason, that, commencing with the right foot at the bottom, the worshipper would find the same foot foremost when he entered the temple, which was considered as a fortunate omen. But the fact is, that the symbolism of numbers was borrowed by the Masons from Pythagoras, in whose system of philosophy it plays an important part, and in which odd numbers were considered as more perfect than even ones. Hence, throughout the masonic system we find a predominance of odd numbers; and while three, five, seven, nine, fifteen, and twenty-seven, are all-important symbols, we seldom find a reference to two, four, six, eight, or ten. The odd number of the stairs was therefore intended to symbolize the idea of perfection, to which it was the object of the aspirant to attain.

As to the particular number of the stairs, this has varied at different periods. Tracing-boards of the last century have been found, in which only *five* steps are delineated, and others in which they amount to *seven*. The Prestonian lectures, used in England in the beginning of this century, gave the whole number as thirty-eight, dividing them into series of one, three, five, seven, nine, and eleven. The error of making an even number, which was a violation of the Pythagorean principle of odd numbers as the symbol of perfection, was corrected in the Hemming lectures, adopted at the union of the two Grand Lodges of England, by striking out the eleven, which was also objectionable as receiving a sectarian explanation. In this country the number was still further reduced to *fifteen*, divided into three series of *three, five,* and *seven*. I shall adopt this

American division in explaining the symbolism, although, after all, the particular number of the steps, or the peculiar method of their division into series, will not in any way affect the general symbolism of the whole legend.

The candidate, then, in the second degree of Masonry, represents a man starting forth on the journey of life, with the great task before him of self-improvement. For the faithful performance of this task, a reward is promised, which reward consists in the development of all his intellectual faculties, the moral and spiritual elevation of his character, and the acquisition of truth and knowledge. Now, the attainment of this moral and intellectual condition supposes an elevation of character, an ascent from a lower to a higher life, and a passage of toil and difficulty, through rudimentary instruction, to the full fruition of wisdom. This is therefore beautifully symbolized by the Winding Stairs; at whose foot the aspirant stands ready to climb the toilsome steep, while at its top is placed "that hieroglyphic bright which none but Craftsmen ever saw," as the emblem of divine truth. And hence a distinguished writer has said that "these steps, like all the masonic symbols, are illustrative of discipline and doctrine, as well as of natural, mathematical, and metaphysical science, and open to us an extensive range of moral and speculative inquiry."

The candidate, incited by the love of virtue and the desire of knowledge, and eager for the reward of truth which is set before him, begins at once the toilsome ascent. At each division he pauses to gather instruction from the symbolism which these divisions present to his attention.

At the first pause which he makes he is instructed in the peculiar organization of the order of which he has become a disciple. But the information here given, if taken in its naked, literal sense, is barren, and unworthy of his labor. The rank of the officers who govern, and the names of the degrees which constitute the institution, can give him no knowledge which he has not before possessed. We must look therefore to the symbolic meaning of these allusions for any value which may be attached to this part of the ceremony.

The reference to the organization of the masonic institution is intended to remind the aspirant of the union of men in society, and the development of the social state out of the state of nature. He is thus reminded, in the very outset of his journey, of the blessings which arise from civilization, and of the fruits of virtue and knowledge which are derived from that condition. Masonry itself is the result of civilization; while, in grateful return, it has been one of the most important means of extending that condition of mankind.

All the monuments of antiquity that the ravages of time have left, combine to prove that man had no sooner emerged from the savage into the social state, than he commenced the organization of religious mysteries, and the separation, by a sort of divine instinct, of the sacred from the profane. Then came the invention of architecture as a means of providing convenient dwellings and necessary shelter from the inclemencies and vicissitudes of the seasons, with all the mechanical arts connected with it; and lastly, geometry, as a necessary science to enable the cultivators of land to measure and designate the limits of their possessions. All these are claimed as peculiar characteristics of Speculative Masonry, which may be considered as the type of civilization, the former bearing the same relation to the profane world as the latter does to the savage state. Hence we at once see the fitness of the symbolism which commences the aspirant's upward progress in the cultivation of knowledge and the search after truth, by recalling to his mind the condition of civilization and the social union of mankind as necessary preparations for the attainment of these objects. In the allusions to the officers of a lodge, and the degrees of Masonry as explanatory of the organization of our own society, we clothe in our symbolic language the history of the organization of society.

Advancing in his progress, the candidate is invited to contemplate another series of instructions. The human senses, as the appropriate channels through which we receive all our ideas of perception, and which, therefore, constitute the most important sources of our knowledge, are here referred to as a symbol of intellectual cultivation. Architecture, as the most important of the arts which conduce to the comfort of mankind, is also alluded to here, not simply because it is so closely connected with the operative institution of Masonry, but also as the type of all the other useful arts. In his second pause, in the ascent of the Winding Stairs, the aspirant is therefore reminded of the necessity of cultivating practical knowledge.

So far, then, the instructions he has received relate to his own condition in society as a member of the great social compact, and to his means of becoming, by a knowledge of the arts of practical life, a necessary and useful member of that society.

But his motto will be, "Excelsior." Still must he go onward and forward. The stair is still before him; its summit is not yet reached, and still further treasures of wisdom are to be sought for, or the reward will not be gained, nor the *middle chamber*, the abiding place of truth, be reached.

In his third pause, he therefore arrives at that point in which the whole circle of human science is to be explained. Symbols, we know, are in themselves arbitrary and of conventional signification, and the complete circle of human science might have been as well symbolized by any other sign or series of doctrines as by the seven liberal arts and sciences. But Masonry is an institution of the olden time; and this selection of the liberal arts and sciences as a symbol of the completion of human learning is one of the most pregnant evidences that we have of its antiquity.

In the seventh century, and for a long time afterwards, the circle of instruction to which all the learning of the most eminent schools and most distinguished philosophers was confined, was limited to what were then called the liberal arts and sciences, and consisted of two branches, the *trivium* and the *quadrivium*. The *trivium* included grammar, rhetoric, and logic; the *quadrivium* comprehended arithmetic, geometry, music, and astronomy.

"These seven heads," says Enfield, "were supposed to

include universal knowledge. He who was master of these was thought to have no need of a preceptor to explain any books or to solve any questions which lay within the compass of human reason, the knowledge of the *trivium* having furnished him with the key to all language, and that of the *quadrivium* having opened to him the secret laws of nature."

At a period, says the same writer, when few were instructed in the *trivium*, and very few studied the *quadrivium*, to be master of both was sufficient to complete the character of a philosopher. The propriety, therefore, of adopting the seven liberal arts and sciences as a symbol of the completion of human learning is apparent. The candidate, having reached this point, is now supposed to have accomplished the task upon which he had entered—he has reached the last step, and is now ready to receive the full fruition of human learning.

So far, then, we are able to comprehend the true symbolism of the Winding Stairs. They represent the progress of an inquiring mind with the toils and labors of intellectual cultivation and study, and the preparatory acquisition of all human science, as a preliminary step to the attainment of divine truth, which it must be remembered is always symbolized in Masonry by the WORD.

Here let me again allude to the symbolism of numbers, which is for the first time presented to the consideration of the masonic student in the legend of the Winding Stairs. The theory of numbers as the symbols of certain qualities was originally borrowed by the Masons from the school of Pythagoras. It will be impossible, however, to develop this doctrine, in its entire extent, on the present occasion, for the numeral symbolism of Masonry would itself constitute materials for an ample essay. It will be sufficient to advert to the fact that the total number of the steps, amounting in all to *fifteen*, in the American system, is a significant symbol. For *fifteen* was a sacred number among the Orientals, because the letters of the holy name JAH, יה, were, in their numerical value, equivalent to fifteen; and hence a figure in which the nine digits were so disposed as to make fifteen either way when added together perpendicularly, horizontally, or diagonally, constituted one of their most sacred talismans. The fifteen steps in the Winding Stairs are therefore symbolic of the name of God.

But we are not yet done. It will be remembered that a reward was promised for all this toilsome ascent of the Winding Stairs. Now, what are the wages of a Speculative Mason? Not money, nor corn, nor wine, nor oil. All these are but symbols. His wages are TRUTH, or that approximation to it which will be most appropriate to the degree into which he has been initiated. It is one of the most beautiful, but at the same time most abstruse, doctrines of the science of masonic symbolism, that the Mason is ever to be in search of truth, but is never to find it. This divine truth, the object of all his labors, is symbolized by the WORD, for which we all know he can only obtain a *substitute*; and this is intended to teach the humiliating but necessary lesson that the knowledge of the nature of God and of man's relation to him, which knowledge constitutes divine truth, can never be acquired in this life. It is only when the portals of the grave open to us, and give us an entrance into a more perfect life, that this knowledge is to be attained. "Happy is the man," says the father of lyric poetry, "who descends beneath the hollow earth, having beheld these mysteries; he knows the end, he knows the origin of life."

The Middle Chamber is therefore symbolic of this life, where the symbol only of the word can be given, where the truth is to be reached by approximation only, and yet where we are to learn that that truth will consist in a perfect knowledge of the G.A.O.T.U. This is the reward of the inquiring Mason; in this consist the wages of a Fellow Craft; he is directed to the truth, but must travel farther and ascend still higher to attain it.

It is, then, as a symbol, and a symbol only, that we must study this beautiful legend of the Winding Stairs. If we attempt to adopt it as an historical fact, the absurdity of its details stares us in the face, and wise men will wonder at our credulity. Its inventors had no desire thus to impose upon our folly; but offering it to us as a great philosophical myth, they did not for a moment suppose that we would pass over its sublime moral teachings to accept the allegory as an historical narrative, without meaning, and wholly irreconcilable with the records of Scripture, and opposed by all the principles of probability. To suppose that eighty thousand craftsmen were weekly paid in the narrow precincts of the temple chambers, is simply to suppose an absurdity. But to believe that all this pictorial representation of an ascent by a Winding Staircase to the place where the wages of labor were to be received, was an allegory to teach us the ascent of the mind from ignorance, through all the toils of study and the difficulties of obtaining knowledge, receiving here a little and there a little, adding something to the stock of our ideas at each step, until, in the middle chamber of life,—in the full fruition of manhood,—the reward is attained, and the purified and elevated intellect is invested with the reward in the direction how to seek God and God's truth,—to believe this is to believe and to know the true design of Speculative Masonry, the only design which makes it worthy of a good or a wise man's study.

Its historical details are barren, but its symbols and allegories are fertile with instruction.

The Third Degree:
Its Ornaments and Emblems

PREFACE

The success which attended my little volume "THE COMPLETE MANUAL OF FREEMASONRY", led me to prepare this Address. Freemasons over all the world regard the Third Degree as one that is high and sublime in the truest sense of these words. It is a beautiful Degree, rich in ceremonial, every part of which is instinct with meaning. But justice is seldom done to it. In some Lodges the Lecture is omitted; in other Lodges the Ornaments are overlooked, or the Emblems left unexplained. These things should never be forgotten, and the aim of the following pages is to present the main feature of the Lecture together with the meaning and symbolism of the Ornaments and Emblems, and the leading thoughts in the concluding Charge in one comprehensive Address.

I want to explain that while the form may be original the matter is not wholly new. I have gone to the great minds of the past and drawn whatever I thought might be of service to the Freemason of to-day. I am glad to learn that what I have done has received commendation, and that the following pages have been incorporated into the recognized Ritual of many Lodges. Right Worshipful Masters who adopt the following Lecture should us the "Short Raising" as it appears in my "Complete Manual", and substituting this Lecture for the "Charge After Raising", which is given in that handbook.

The Third Degree: Its Ornaments And Emblems

By William Harvey

Sir, - The observant brother who completes the Masonic circle by reaching the High and Sublime Degree of Master, cannot fail to notice that the great purpose of our Fraternity is to advance the destiny of the race by deepening the spirit of brotherhood, ennobling humanity, and establishing truth and righteousness in all the world.

In future years you may journey far along our mystic paths in a praiseworthy desire to add to your knowledge of our ancient Craft, but I venture to say that nothing you may hereafter learn will add to the simple dignity of the structure, the plan of which is now revealed to your gaze, and in the building of which I invite you to become a fellow-worker with all those in whose footsteps you have travelled tonight.

As Freemasons, drawing our inspiration from those sermons in stones which rose to the music of the mallet and chisel of our early operative Brethren, we look backward along the corridor of time, and conjure up the mighty fane that was raised by Israel's King to Israel's god, and, taking that as the symbol of our faith, we seek to build a temple in the hearts of men. Its foundation are laid in our common brotherhood; its walls are raised in our mutual sympathies and kindred needs; its pillars are fashioned out of purity and truth; its altar is fear of

God and love of our fellow-men; and its chief oblation is a heart aglow with the desire of doing good.

He who would build well must have a keen appreciation of the value of time, and recognize that every moment is a precious jewel not to be wasted nor thrown lightly away. Therefore it is meet that in these emblems of mortality that lie around, the Hourglass should occupy a place of prominence. Down through the centuries this simple device has been used as a means of measuring Time, and in the age-long process has come to be regarded as a fitting symbol of human life. You remember what the poet says?

> *A handful of red sand from the hot clime*
> *Of Arab deserts brought,*
> *Within this Glass becomes the Spy of Time,*
> *The Minister of Thought.*

As the Hourglass is a symbol of human life, so the Scythe is an emblem of time. Artists, seeking to give form and feature to the advancing years of the world, have pictured time as a man grey in service and wise with experience who, in calm serenity of mind and purpose, is forever employed in gathering the harvest of this mortal life unto the vast storehouse of Eternity. And how uncertain is the time of harvest for all of us! It is but a commonplace of speech to say that the sun may never rise again for you or me. Ere the sawn we may be numbered with the countless millions who have laid down the working-tools of life for ever. But even this very uncertainty of time should be an incentive to us so to use our days that when we pass into that Silent Land were Death is King, we shall leave a name untarnished and beloved. It matters not how long we live, but how.

We live in deeds, not years; in thoughts, not breaths;
In feelings, not in figures on a dial.
We should count time by heart throbs. He most lives
Who thinks most, feels the noblest, acts the best.

The emblems of human life and Time - the Hourglass and the Scythe - to which I have drawn your attention, are fitly associated with the Checkered Pavement, which is patterned on the floor of every Lodge. According to the Masonic tradition, it was thus that the pavement of the great Temple of Solomon was adorned, and the striking arrangement of stones having passed into our scheme of moral symbolism, has become an emblem of character. The white squares and the black at once suggest Good and Evil, Light and Darkness, Heaven and Hell. The choice lies before each of us; our lives are in our hands to make them what we will; but if our Masonic system be of any value - if it have any influence - then surely shall we follow after Good and forsake Evil, seek light and eschew Darkness, and so play our parts in building the moral Temple of the Universe, that our feet shall ever be kept in the narrow path of rectitude that leads at last to Heaven.

Let us meditate, therefore, upon our days and the swiftness of their passing. Even now as we linger, the running sands are carrying with them the moments of our lives into the eternity of the past, each with its tale of good or evil, its record of things done or undone. And no moment ever returns.

As the Persian philosopher phrases it?

The Moving Finger writes; and having writ
 Moves on; nor all they Piety nor Wit
Shall lure it back to cancel half a Line;
 Nor all they Tears wash out a word of it.

How imperative it is, therefore, that we should realize the mission to which, as Freemasons, we are called. To soothe calamity, alleviate misfortune, compassionate misery, and restore peace to the troubled mind is our grand aim. On this basis we establish our friendships and form our connections.

We recognize that the Universe has not been provided as a mere plaything for Man, but that Man was created to carry out certain labors in obedience to the divine Will. And the Great Architect of the Universe lays down the lines upon which that work shall become effective. All the Masonic virtues are means by which God makes our lives enrich Society and the World, and therefore, as faithful workers in the design of our Grand Master, it is our bounden duty to devote every moment to the one supreme task of making

This life, as best we can,
Devoid of suffering, pain, heartache,
A present heaven for man.

By the thoughts, words and actions of our daily lives we are builders - or it may be destroyers - of the Temple, to the erection of which we are called, and when, at the touch of the grim Tyler of Eternity, we lay down the mallet and chisel, Time - merciless but just - will reckon with what measure of success we have built or destroyed. Therefore, my brother –

> *Redeem the hours while in they Glass*
>   *The Sands in silence run;*
> *Too soon the day of life will pass*
>   *Too soon the sunset gun*
> *Will sound, and summon thee to rest*
>   *And all thy work be done.*

If, as the last sands run out and the shadows fall around, you are permitted to dwell for a moment on the record of your days, surely there shall be peace in your heart, if the exclamation of the poet may truthfully be yours –

> *And when the precious hours are done,*
> *How sweet at set of sun*
> *To gather up the fair laborious day!*
> *To have struck some blow for right*
> *With tongue or pen;*
> *To have smoothed the path to light*
> *For wandering men!*
> *To have chased some mighty fiend of Ill away!*

The Coffin, Skull and Cross bones are emblems of the inevitable destiny of our mortal bodies. As we stand in the presence of these grim reminders of decay and dissolution, let us meditate for a moment upon Death and all that it portends.

> *Behold this ruin; 'tis a skull*
> *Once of ethereal spirit full;*
> *This narrow cell was Life's retreat,*
> *This space was Thought's mysterious seat;*
> *What beauteous visions filled this spot,*
> *What dreams of pleasure long forgot,*
> *Nor hope, nor joy, nor love, nor fear,*
> *Hath left one trace of record here.*
>
> *Beneath this mold'ring canopy*
> *Once shone a bright and busy eye,*
> *But start not at the dismal void —*
> *If social love that eye employed,*
> *If with no lawless fires it gleamed,*
> *But through the dews of kindness beamed,*
> *That eye shall be for ever bright*
> *When sun and stars are sunk in night.*
>
> *Within this hollow cavern, hung*
> *The ready, swift and tuneful tongue;*
> *If falsehood's honey is disdained,*
> *And, where it could not praise, was chained;*
> *If bold in virtue's cause it spoke,*
> *Yet gentle concord never broke,*
> *That silent tongue will plead for thee*
> *When Time unveils Eternity.*

An Eastern proverb says that Death is a black camel which kneels at every door, and our Masonic teaching adopts the Level as the symbol of death, which is the grand Leveler of all human greatness.

The prince who kept the world in awe,
The judge whose dictate fixed the law,
The rich, the poor, the great, the small
Are leveled; Death confounds them all.

In the presence of Death what are the externals of majesty, the pride of wealth, or the charms of beauty? View life stripped of her ornaments and exposed in her natural meanness, and you will be convinced of the futility of these empty delusions. In the grave all fallacies are detected, all ranks leveled, and all distinctions done away.

But in spite of the mementoes of mortality with which we daily meet, and notwithstanding the fact that Death has established his empire over all the works of nature, we are apt to forget that we are born to die. We go on from one design to another, adding hope to hope, and laying out plans for the employment of many years, till we are suddenly alarmed with the approach of Death when we least expect him, and at an hour which, amidst the gaieties of life, we probably conclude to be the very meridian of our existence.

As life is uncertain, and all earthly pursuits vain, no man should postpone the important concern of preparing for eternity. Rather should we all hasten to embrace the happy moment, while time and opportunity offer to provide against the great change, when the pleasures of the world shall cease to delight, and the reflections of a virtuous mind yield the only comfort and consolation. Our hopes will not then be frustrated, nor shall we be hurried, unprepared, into the presence of the All Wise and Omnipotent Judge, to Whom the secrets of all hearts are known, and from Whose dread tribunal no culprit can escape.

As, therefore, you have been taught at every step of your Masonic career your duty to God, to your neighbor, and to yourself, you should support with propriety the character of our profession, advert to the nature of our solemnities, and, with assiduity, pursue the sacred tenets of our Order.

Strive to adorn the symbolic jewels of a Master Mason, which are Friendship, Morality, and Brotherly Love. These should ever be an adornment to your mind - Morality being practical virtue and the duty of life; friendship that personal kindness which extends from the center of private connections to the circle of universal philanthropy; and Brotherly Love, the purest emanation of earthly friendship. The desire of power in excess caused the Angels to fall; the desire of knowledge in excess caused Man to fall; but in Brotherly Love there is no excess, neither can angel or man come in danger by it. It is the foundation and copestone, the cement and glory of our Ancient Fraternity.

By its exercise you are taught to regard the whole human species as one family, the high and the low, the rich and the poor who, as children of the same parent, are to aid, support, and protect each other. On this principle Freemasonry unites men of every country, sect, or opinion; and conciliates true friendship among those who might otherwise have remained at a perpetual distance. By the study of our emblems and the practice of our precepts may you, as a child of Light, be enabled through Divine aid to turn from works of Darkness, Obscenity, Drunkenness, and all manner of Evil, and live in the daily practice of Charity, Benevolence, Justice, Temperance, Chastity, and Brotherly Love. Ever bear in mind that Virtue is true nobility, and that Wisdom is the channel by which Virtue is directed and conveyed. Wisdom and Virtue are the only qualities that are permitted to mark distinction among Freemasons. With becoming reverence supplicate the divine aid of the Great Architect of the Universe, by Whose favor and under Whose protection you may be permitted to excel in both, and thus, when the awful moment arrives when Death shall raise his warning finger, you will enter without dread or apprehension upon that journey to the country whence no traveler returns.

> *Death cannot come*
> *To him untimely who is fit to die;*
> *The less of this cold world, the more of Heaven;*
> *The briefer life, the earlier immortality.*

But - and this is one of the great purposes of the third Degree - while Death is ever near, riding on every passing breeze, and lurking in every flower, still, in the truest sense,

There is no Death! What seems so is a transition.
This life of mortal breath
Is but a suburb of the life Elysian.

All men desire to be immortal, and there is in the minds of men, whatever their religion or want of religion, a certain presage of a future existence, and this takes the deepest root and is most discoverable in the greatest geniuses and most exalted souls. One of the ornaments of a Master Mason's Lodge is the Porch, which was the entrance to the Sanctum Sanctorum, or Holy of Holies, and this, to the meditative Mason, symbolizes the grave through which all must pass. The grave is but the gate that leads to a larger and full live - is but the passing from darkness to light, from the uncertain gloom of time to the unsullied radiance of Eternity, or, in the language of our Masonic Art, is by the close-tyled door that leads to the Celestial Lodge over which the Grand Master Himself presides, and in which there is an honored place for all those who have been faithful here. Other Emblems of our Faith are instinct with lessons of similar import. To the thoughtful Mason, the Spade denotes that this world is but the tilling-ground of Heaven; the Anchor is the emblem of a well-grounded hope in a glorious immortality, when the frail bark of life shall be moored for ever to the shore of that fadeless land whether the wicked cease from troubling and the weary are at rest; and the Sprig of Acacia, as an evergreen, is a fitting emblem of the immortal soul which never dies. All combine in the third Degree, my Brother, to teach you to look beyond the narrow limits of this world, and to see man raised from the grave of iniquity, by faith and the grace of god, to everlasting life and blessedness. By the light of the Divine Countenance you may pass without trembling through the gloomy mansions of the dead, where all the things of life are forgotten; and when, having fought a good fight here, you stand at the Bar of divine Justice to receive your reward, you will most surely realize that,

> *It is not death to die*
> *To leave this weary road,*
> *And with the brotherhood on high*
> *To be at home with God.*

And now, my brother, having by the ceremonial through which you have gone won your place as a Master Mason among these friends and brethren of your Mother Lodge, let me, in conclusion, address a few words to those who constitutes the Lodge within whose walls you have now a place.

Brethren, surrounded thus by these emblems of dissolution, let us, ere we return with our young Brother to the outer world, resolve anew to mark our superiority and distinction among men by the sincerity of our profession as Freemasons. The Masonic virtues are those upon which Society is based. The Masonic ideals are those of pure and aspiring humanity. The Masonic life is the spirit in which families cling to each other, citizens adhere to each, class has intercourse with class. Let us never forget that Freemasonry has no room for the man who places money above honor, selfishness above righteousness, passion above virtue, power and place above manhood and integrity.

Within these sacred walls may we enjoy every satisfaction and delight which disinterested friendship can give and, as a result of our meeting from time to time, may we become increasingly influential in spreading the light of Wisdom, aiding the strength of Reason, dispensing the beauty of Virtue, and lessening the sum of human misery and vice. May we be taught to measure our actions by the rule of rectitude, square our conduct by the principles of morality, and keep our thoughts within the circle of propriety. Let us cultivate the moral virtue and improve in all that is good and amiable. Let the genius of Masonry preside over our conduct, and under her sway let us perform our part with becoming dignity. Let us preserve an elevation of understanding, a politeness of manner, and an evenness of temper; let our recreations be innocent and pursued with moderation, and never let irregular indulgences lead to the subversion of our system by impairing our faculties, or exposing our character to derision. In conformity to our precepts, as patterns worthy of imitation, let the respectability of our character be supported by the regularity of our conduct and the uniformity of our deportment. Then, as citizens of the world, and friends to every clime, we shall be living examples of virtue and benevolence, equally zealous to merit as to obtain universal approbation. In such wise shall we be true and good Masons, faithful in our imitation of the celebrated artist whose unshaken fidelity and noble death have once again been represented to us. By such exemplary conduct we shall convince the world that merit is the only title to our privileges, and that the favors of Freemasonry are not undeservedly bestowed.

As forth we stand on every briary path,
    We know that in the ages long gone by
Each bitter toil did find its aftermath
    In laurels green, and lives that never die.
And therefore journey, therefore patient build
    Our nation and ourselves. With workful prayer,
Cementing well each joint as Heaven-willed,
    Submitting all to God's great perfect square.
And as we labor on the quarried stone,
    And wall, and join each course to Heaven's plan
We see that 'gainst the deep, blue sky is thrown
    The Temple, symbol of Completed Man.

Soliloquy For a Master Mason

Tis yonder from Mount Moriah I have come, filled with soulful remorse, not knowing whether it is better to tarry or to flee. But, hist! I am nearing the spot of the present concealment of the body, after having prepared a place to hide more completely from human sight forever the victim of our crime. Dreaming visions of the past, the present and the future are flying through my distracted brain; but I will tarry here and await the appointed hour, for the horrid deed is done! Here, cold and mute, wrapped in the icy cloak of death, the Master sleeps. No more the pomp and pageantry of power; no more the many craftsmen hurrying hither and thither to do his deep designs. Yet under the direction of the masterful mind, the Temple in all its grandeur and beauty has arisen, towering over the hills and beckoning the heavens to rest upon it's stately columns. No more shall this, his high ambition gratify.

Oh death, untimely! Yet, oh timely death! Wrestled from life while fresh his honors cluster; before the fetid breath of calumny had marred the splendor of his name, or slander smirched the glory of his achievements. He has fallen, yielding up his life rather than break his vows; surrendering all that the world holds-power, riches, life itself, yet holding fast to his Masonic secret.

Oh, integrity most rare! Oh, fortitude most grand! To him in future years shall countless Masons raise songs of praise to laud his name. Oh, death preferred, rather than faithless prove, rather than trust betray. Yet, though well kept, his secret is revealed. I read it thus: The secret of a Master Mason is contained in these three words: Truth, Honor, and Fortitude.

(Low twelve bell strikes.)

But, hark! The tuneful bells ring out the hour of meeting; but where are my accomplices in crime? Oh, ye Gods! Must I alone, in the gloom of the midnight hour, in ghostly presence come?

www.ingramcontent.com/pod-product-compliance
Lightning Source LLC
LaVergne TN
LVHW041457070426
835507LV00009B/655